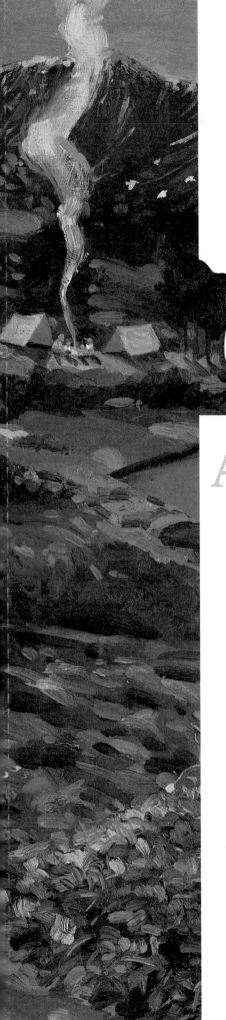

TREASUR

MW01094908

PRACTICE BOOK

A PLACE TO DREAM

HARCOURT BRACE & COMPANY

Orlando   Atlanta   Austin   Boston   San Francisco   Chicago   Dallas   New York
Toronto   London

C O N T E N T S

Printed in the United States of America

ISBN 0-15-301293-5

13 14 15   030   01 2000 99

Name _____

Read the story. Use clues in the story to decide what each underlined word means. Write each word next to its meaning.

I was looking at pictures of things for sale in some old <u>catalogues</u> in our attic. Out of one book fell a picture of my great-grandfather.

I was very eager to learn about him. "If you are <u>curious</u> about him," my mother said, "read this old journal."

I found out that my great-grandfather grew up in the hills and <u>hollows</u> of Tennessee. His father wanted him to be a farmer, but Great-Grandfather became a woodcarver. The first thing he carved was a <u>lupine</u>, a common flower near his home.

Later, Great-Grandfather carved <u>figureheads</u> for the fronts of sailing ships. His figureheads sailed from frozen, northern shores to hot, <u>tropical</u> lands. Making beautiful things gave my great-grandfather a feeling of <u>satisfaction</u>.

1. _____ eager to know more

2. _____ small valleys

3. _____ a plant with flowers on spikes

4. _____ carved figures on fronts of ships

5. _____ relating to hot, damp parts of the world

6. _____ books that show and describe things to buy

7. _____ feeling of having what is wanted or needed

Name _____

Tell what happened in the story "Miss Rumphius" by filling in the chart below.

	How old she was	Where she lived or traveled	Things she did
Alice	_____ _____	_____ _____	_____ _____
Miss Rumphius	_____ _____ _____	_____ _____ _____ _____ _____	_____ _____ _____ _____ _____
That Crazy Old Lady	_____ _____ _____	_____ _____ _____	_____ _____ _____
The Lupine Lady	_____ _____ _____	_____ _____ _____	_____ _____ _____

Miss Rumphius reached her goals by

1. _____

2. _____

3. _____

Name_____

A. Read the sentences below. Draw a line between each sentence on the left and the sentence on the right that describes it.

My father is a weekend gardener.   It asks something.

Where did I put the lettuce seeds?   It gives an order.

Give me the rake.   It tells something.

What a delicious carrot this is!   It shows strong feeling.

B. Rewrite each sentence below so that it has the correct word order, capitalization, and end mark.

have you seen the beautiful blue blossoms

_____

morning glories are wonderful flowers

_____

the flowers do not pick

_____

SUMMARIZING
the **L**EARNING   A sentence that tells something ends with

_____. A sentence that asks something ends with

_____. A sentence that shows strong feeling ends with

_____. A sentence that gives an order ends with

_____ or _____.

Name _____

Read the paragraphs. Then answer the questions.

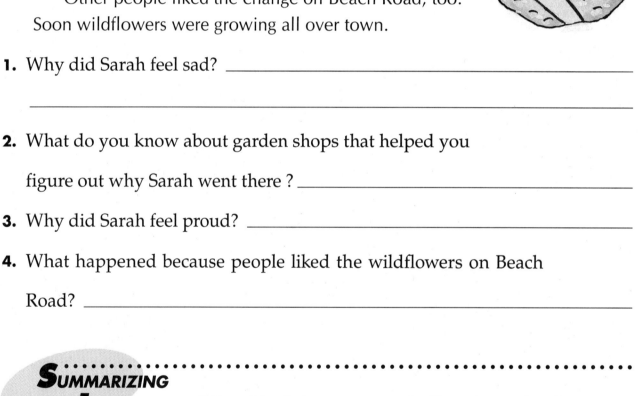

Sarah went for a walk near her new home. The land along Beach Road was empty and brown. Because it was so ugly, Sarah felt sad. Then she had an idea. She would be like Miss Rumphius. She would get some seeds. She walked to the garden shop.

Just a few weeks later, Beach Road looked very different. Colorful wildflowers covered the hills. Every time she looked at them, Sarah felt proud. She had made a difference, all by herself!

Other people liked the change on Beach Road, too. Soon wildflowers were growing all over town.

1. Why did Sarah feel sad? _____

_____

2. What do you know about garden shops that helped you

   figure out why Sarah went there ? _____

3. Why did Sarah feel proud? _____

4. What happened because people liked the wildflowers on Beach

   Road? _____

SUMMARIZING the LEARNING   When I look for causes and effects in stories, I stop and ask two questions.

I ask [_____] **and** [_____]

Name _____

Be an active reader. Fill in the thought balloons before, during, and after your reading of this story. For each box, read as far as the arrow. Then stop and complete the statement.

> Before I read the story, I will

> I think the story might be about

Project Beautiful

"Sometimes Ms. Howard makes my head tired," Jackson said.

"Yeah," said Ronnie. "She sure does make us think a lot."

> This reminds me of

> I wonder

"But I wouldn't swap her for any other teacher in school," Carrie said.

"Me neither."

"Me neither."

Ms. Howard's class had just read "Miss Rumphius." Now the students were working in teams. Each team had to come up with a plan to make something more beautiful.

Jackson, Ronnie, and Carrie were a team. So far, nobody had any ideas. They were sitting in the field behind Guy's Variety Store. There were a few tree stumps that made good chairs.

> I think that

> In my mind, I can picture

I predict

_____

will have a good idea.

In my mind, the field is

My predictions about what would happen were

_____

because

Nobody said anything for a long time. Then Carrie took a paper straw out of her mouth. Chewing it seemed to help her think.

"Okay," she said. "What's beautiful? I think Miss Rumphius was right," she added. "Flowers."

"A sleek jet plane!" Ronnie shouted. He jumped up and zoomed around the tree stumps a few times.

"Animals," Jackson said, "like tigers and polar bears."

Carrie looked at the boys. How would they ever agree on a project?

"Well," she asked, "what's ugly?"

"This field," Jackson said. They looked around. Soda cans littered the overgrown grass. Someone had thrown old tires in a heap. The fence on one side was leaning at a crazy angle.

"You're right," Carrie said.

Ronnie stuck his thumb up and nodded.

The three kids looked at each other.

One by one, they began to grin. They had their project!

I understand. What is happening is

I can imagine what will happen next:

I would/would not (circle one) like to read more of the story because

Name _____

Read the words in the box and the cartoons. Then write each word where it belongs in the cartoons.

exaggerated	**pioneer**	**settlers**
orchard	**recollections**	**wilderness**

Gee, you were the first person to explore this land! Isn't being a _____ scary?

Oh, no, child! Those tall tales you've heard are greatly _____. There is very little danger here in the untamed _____.

Grandmother, I know that the _____ who first farmed this land were your great-grandparents. Did they plant this beautiful _____ of apple trees?

Oh, yes, dear. They wrote their _____ in a memory book! Apple picking has come a long way since then!

Name _____

Think about the story "Johnny Appleseed." Fill in the first two columns before you read. Add to the second column during reading. Fill in the last column after you finish reading the story.

K	W	L
What I Know	*What I Want to Know*	*What I Learned*

Name_____

Read the words. Use the words to make two new words. Write the compound words in the boxes, and then draw pictures to show what the compound words mean.

shoe   horse   lace

_____	_____

wheel   arm   chair

_____	_____

saw   pan   dust

_____	_____

Write a sentence. Use two of your compound words.

_____

_____

Name_____

A. Read the paragraph below. Circle the subject in each sentence.

The rain helped the apple trees grow. Tiny apples grew on the tree. People came to pick the apples. The ripe apples were sweet.

B. Add a subject and an end mark to complete each sentence below. Write your sentence on the line.

chop down the trees

_____

is made from wood

_____

sleeps in a tree

_____

Write a sentence about something in nature that you like. Make sure the sentence has a subject.

_____

_____

SUMMARIZING *the* **L**EARNING   The _____ tells the person or thing the sentence is about. The subject is usually found at the _____ of a sentence.

Name _____

Read the directions for making apple tree art. Then
answer the questions below.

Place your arm and hand on a sheet of paper. Spread out
your fingers. Trace around your hand and up and down your
arm. On your paper, paint the arm part brown for a tree trunk.
Dip a small sponge in green paint. Dab on the leaves. Wait for
the paint to dry. Then cut a small carrot in half. Dip the round
end in red paint. Use it to put the apples on your tree.

1. What things do you need to make your apple tree?

_____

_____

2. As you make your tree, when should you stop for a while?

_____

_____

3. Explain how you should place your hand and arm on the paper.

_____

_____

4. If you make this tree, when do you have to be extra careful?

_____

Why? _____

SUMMARIZING
the **L**EARNING   I always read or listen to all the directions before I try

to follow them. If I don't understand them, I can

_____.

Name _____

Read each paragraph. Write the meanings of the underlined words. Then write under "Clues" how you figured out the meaning.

Meaning: _____

_____

_____

Clues: _____

_____

_____

_____

Apples are delectable! They must be, because we gobble up billions of them every year. Some apples are very sweet. Others have a sharp, tart taste.

Meaning: _____

_____

_____

Clues: _____

_____

_____

_____

Meaning: _____

_____

_____

Clues: _____

_____

_____

_____

Did you know that there are thousands of varieties, or kinds, of apples? Some are green. Some are yellow. Some are as crimson as cherries!

Meaning: _____

_____

_____

Clues: _____

_____

_____

_____

Name _____

Meaning:

_____

_____

Clues: _____

_____

_____

_____

_____

Apples grow nearly <u>everywhere</u> throughout the world. They grow best in areas with <u>frigid</u> winters. They seem to like the cold weather.

Meaning:

_____

_____

Clues: _____

_____

_____

_____

_____

_____

Meaning:

_____

_____

Clues: _____

_____

_____

_____

_____

Apples can either be <u>eaten fresh or</u> <u>consumed</u> as yummy pies, applesauce, or apple juice. They are full of vitamins A and C. So eat some apples today! They are <u>unbeatable</u>!

Meaning:

_____

_____

Clues: _____

_____

_____

_____

_____

_____

HBJ material copyrighted under notice appearing earlier in this work.

Practice Book ▪ A PLACE TO DREAM

Structural and Contextual Clues 13

Name_____

Reread these sentences from "Johnny Appleseed."
Then fill in the boxes.

1. John's first years were hard. His father left the family to fight in the
Revolutionary War, and his mother and his baby brother both died before
his second birthday.

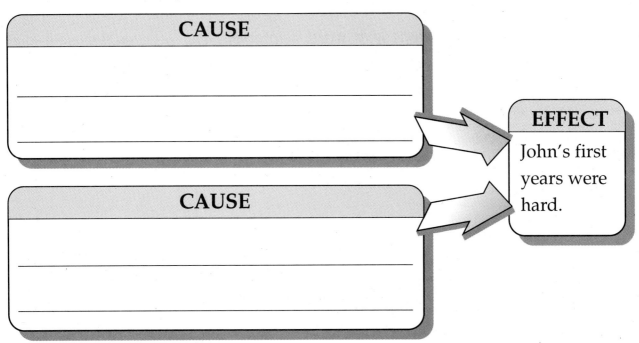

CAUSE

CAUSE

EFFECT

John's first
years were
hard.

2. When Johnny passed seventy, it became difficult for him to keep up with his
work. Then, in March of 1845, while trudging through a snowstorm near
Fort Wayne, Indiana, he became ill for the first time in his life. Johnny asked
for shelter in a settler's cabin, and a few days later he died there.

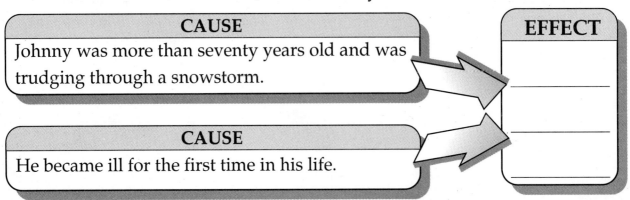

CAUSE

Johnny was more than seventy years old and was
trudging through a snowstorm.

CAUSE

He became ill for the first time in his life.

EFFECT

Name_____

Rosita is reading about growing apples. She needs help taking notes and writing a summary of what she has read. First, read the paragraphs below. Then help Rosita fill in her notebook.

Starting new plants is called propagation. Most new apple trees are propagated from buds. A tree twig with a bud is cut from a healthy tree and *grafted,* or attached, to another tree. The tree will grow the same kind of apples as the tree from which the bud is cut.

Young apple trees are planted about thirty feet apart. That allows room for farmers to spray them for insects and to *prune* them. Pruning is cutting back some of the branches so that the tree will produce better fruit.

Apple farmers have to work hard and be patient. It takes from three to ten years for a young apple tree to start producing delicious apples.

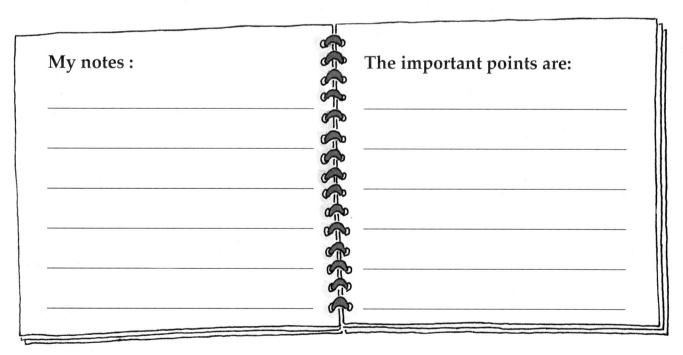

My notes :

The important points are:

Name_____

Read this story. Then read the story again, and as you
read, write the most important points on the "Notes" page.

Some of the tales people told
about Johnny Appleseed described
the clothes he wore. Instead of a
shirt he wore a cloth sack, cutting
holes for his head and arms. Some
said he wore a frying pan for a hat.

Johnny never cared much for
shoes. He often went barefoot, and
years of walking made his feet very

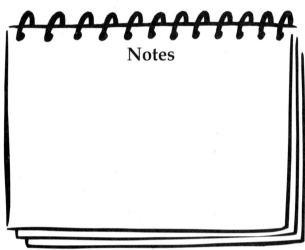

tough. Once, during a snowstorm, a man gave Johnny a pair of shoes and
insisted he wear them. Johnny did, but not for long. When he met a man who
needed the shoes even more than he did, he gave them away.

What would you tell Rosita about the story? Give her a summary of it,
including only the most important points.

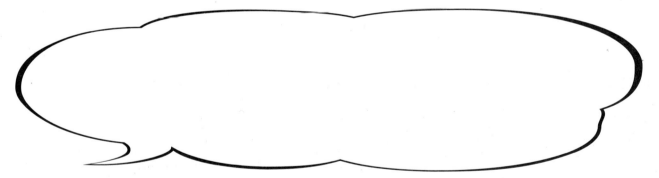

Choose a story about Johnny Appleseed, Paul Bunyan, John Henry, or
Pecos Bill from your library. As you read it, take notes about the most
important points. Then tell your classmates what happened in the story.

Name_____

Read the words in the box. Think about their meanings.
Then write each word where it belongs.

explore	**exciting**	**adventures**
treasure	**assigned**	**apartment**

1. A family might live in this instead of a house. _____

2. It would be _____ to solve a mystery!

3. Pirates often hid their _____ in a chest.

4. Travel can be full of thrilling _____.

5. This word rhymes with *before*. _____

6. Last week our teacher _____ a book report.

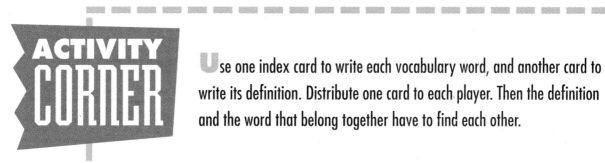

ACTIVITY CORNER

Use one index card to write each vocabulary word, and another card to write its definition. Distribute one card to each player. Then the definition and the word that belong together have to find each other.

THE ADVENTURES OF ALI BABA BERNSTEIN ● ● ●

Name_____

Complete the story frame to tell what happens in "The Adventures of Ali Baba Bernstein."

"The Adventures of Ali Baba Bernstein" takes place in the city of

_____. It is about a boy whose real name is

_____. He decides to change his name to _____,

because _____

_____.

    A problem begins when Ali Baba finds _____

in the basement of his apartment building. He decides that this

belongs to _____. Then he hears what he thinks is

_____.

However, he finds out that the sound is really _____.

Mr. _____ invites Ali Baba to _____

_____.

Would you like to read more about Ali Baba's adventures? Write a sentence telling why or why not.

_____

_____

Name_____

A. Read the paragraph below. Underline the predicate in each sentence.

Ali Baba Bernstein went down to the basement. He looked in his family's storage cage. A shoebox slid across the floor! Ali Baba jumped onto a chair. A cat jumped out from the box.

B. Add a predicate and an end mark to complete each sentence below. Write your sentence on the line.

David Bernstein _____

Mrs. Booxbaum _____

The librarian _____

Mr. Vivaldi _____

Write two sentences about something special you have found. Make sure each sentence has a predicate.

_____

_____

_____

•••

SUMMARIZING
the **L**EARNING   The _____ of a sentence tells what the

subject of the sentence is or does.

Name _____

Find the names of twelve shops. Then make a
directory for Ali Baba. Write the shop names in
alphabetical order.

You may want to list the names here first.

_____ _____

_____ _____

_____ _____

_____ _____

_____ _____

_____ _____

TOYLAND

PALS AND PETS VET

CRITTERS PET SHOP

SNOOKY'S SHOES

GIGGLES CARD SHOP

SNIPPY SCISSORS HAIR SALON

PAGES BOOKSHOP

SNACK SHACK DINER

GO ON

Name _____

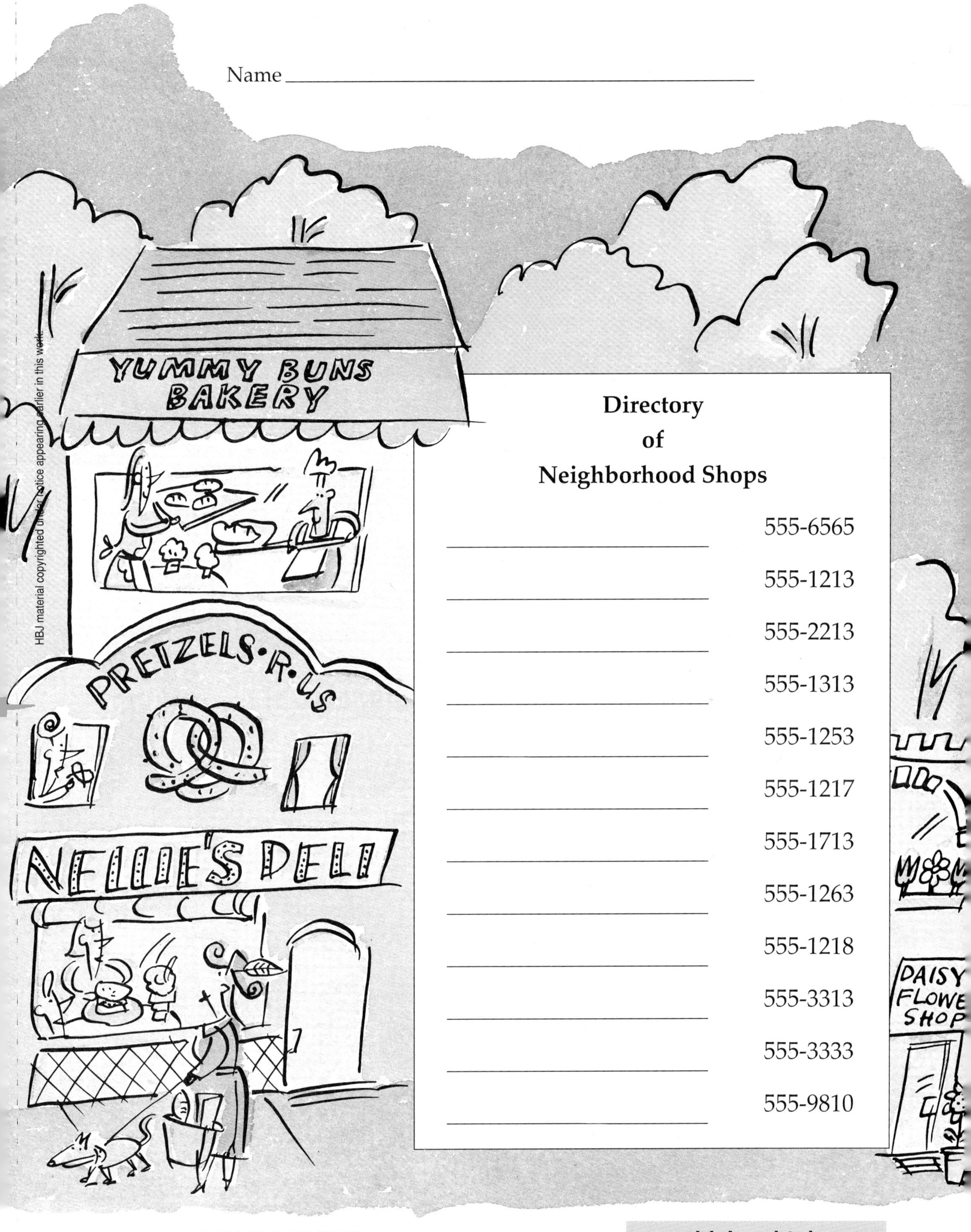

Directory
of
Neighborhood Shops

_____ 555-6565

_____ 555-1213

_____ 555-2213

_____ 555-1313

_____ 555-1253

_____ 555-1217

_____ 555-1713

_____ 555-1263

_____ 555-1218

_____ 555-3313

_____ 555-3333

_____ 555-9810

Name_____

A. Show Rusty the Robot how to use a card catalog.
Look carefully at the card catalog. Write the number
of the drawer he should look in for each book.

1. a book named *Arabian Nights*

2. a book about New York City

3. a book by Johanna Hurwitz

4. the book *What Your Last Name Means*

5. a book about the composer Vivaldi

6. a book about Italy

7. a book about treasure hunters

8. the book *Opera for Young Listeners*

9. a book about Maria Callas

10. a book by Helen Leffert

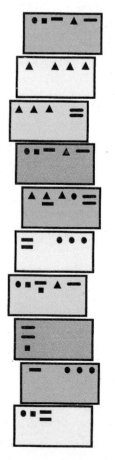

Name _____

B. Rusty has taken the card below from the card catalog. Look at the card. Complete the labels to tell about each part of the card.

This is the _____.

This is the name of _____.

These two lines tell that the book may be found in the

_____

section of the library under the

letter _____.

J
Hurwitz

        Hurwitz, Johanna.

Much Ado About Aldo / Johanna Hurwitz;

Illustrated by John Wallner.

New York: Morrow, ©1978.
-- 1st ed. --

This is the year when

_____.

With a partner, make a poster that explains how to use the card catalog. Display the poster in your classroom or in the library.

Name_____

Get ready for a concert! Write the correct word next to each clue below. The words you will need are coming from the oboe.

Clues

1. What do you call the people who come to hear a concert? _____

2. These are people who play music._____

3. This word describes a sharp high sound. _____

4. This is another word for "beat." _____

5. These are combinations of notes played together. _____

6. The oboe and the flute are two of these. _____

7. This is a group of musicians led by a conductor. _____

With a partner, write a brief story that uses all of the vocabulary words. Then read the story, stopping each time you come to one of the vocabulary words. See how quickly your listeners can fill in the words.

Name_____

A. Write the name of each instrument in "Meet the Orchestra" on the star where it belongs.

_____ _____

STRINGS

_____ _____

WOODWINDS

_____ _____

_____

_____ _____

BRASS

_____

_____

PERCUSSION

_____

B. The most interesting thing I learned about the orchestra is this:

_____

_____

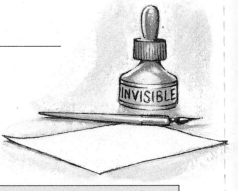

Name_____

Solve the secret message! Use the pronunciation key to figure out what word each respelling stands for. Then write each word where it belongs. The words you need are in the box on the right.

a	add	i	it	oo	took	oi	oil
ā	ace	ī	ice	o͞o	pool	ou	pout
â	care	o	odd	u	up	ng	ring
ä	palm	ō	open	û	burn	th	thin
e	end	ô	order	yo͞o	fuse	t̶h̶	this
ē	equal					zh	vision

ə = { a in *above*   e in *sicken*   i in *possible*
      o in *melon*   u in *circus*

HBJ School Dictionary, Harcourt Brace Jovanovich, 1990

super	**supper**
concert	**orchestra**
corner	**whole**
excitement	

Meet me at the [kôr′nər] _____ of 29th Street and Elm

after [sup′ər] _____. There's going to be a [kon′sûrt]

_____ at the Music Hall. Guess who's playing in

the [ôr′kəs•trə] _____! You're in for a

[so͞o′pər] _____ surprise. The [hōl] _____ town

will be there, so don't miss the [ik•sīt′mənt] _____!

Play "Here's How to Say It." With your classmates, make a list of words from your reading that you don't know how to say. Write each word on one side of an index card, look up the word in a dictionary, and write how to say it on the other side of the card. When you have enough cards, take turns looking at the words and saying them.

Name_____

A. **Read the paragraph. Circle all the common nouns.**

Have you ever seen an orchestra perform? The players sit in different sections on the stage. The conductor leads them. He waves a stick called a baton. The audience watches the conductor and the players.

B. **Read the sentences below. Use the clues to fill in each blank with a common noun to tell a story. Your story can be serious or silly.**

The _____ played a _____ in the _____.
    (person)   (instrument)   (place)

Suddenly, a _____ jumped on the red _____ nearby.
    (animal)   (thing)

A _____ screamed and ran to the _____.
  (person)   (place)

With all the noise, no one could hear the music.

Now, write a sentence about an instrument you would like to play. Use at least two different common nouns.

_____

_____

SUMMARIZING *the* **L**EARNING   A noun that names any _____,

_____, or _____ is called a common noun. Every

_____ begins with a lowercase letter.

Name_____

Read the paragraph below. Think about the main idea
and the details. Then write your responses in the notepad.

Everybody knows that the
conductor waves a baton to keep
the orchestra playing together, but
did you know that the conductor
has other jobs as well? It is usually
the conductor who chooses the
music to be played at a concert.
The conductor must also interpret
the music, or decide exactly how it
should be played. When the
orchestra practices, the conductor
is in charge. He or she asks the
musicians to play parts of the
music over and over again until it
sounds just right.

Write a sentence that sums up
the main idea of the paragraph.

_____

_____

Write three details that support
that main idea.

1. _____

_____

2. _____

_____

3. _____

_____

What are all the details about?

_____

_____

Name_____

Read about Marian Anderson. Then answer the
questions on the next page.

Marian Anderson was a person who just wouldn't
give up. Even though people said, "You will never
make it," her beautiful voice still rang out.

Marian loved music all her life. She began singing
concerts in her church when she was eight years old.
Her family had little money, but Marian still found
voice teachers to help her improve her singing.

After high school, Marian tried to go to a music
school. Sadly, the school took white students only.
Marian kept on singing anyway. She sang for
several years in Europe, where she became
famous. When she returned to America, she gave
more and more concerts, and listeners were
amazed at her beautiful voice. A famous conductor
heard her sing and said, "A voice like hers comes once
in a century."

Marian's most famous concert was in 1939. She
had wanted to sing in Constitution Hall, a concert
hall in Washington, D.C. However, because she was
an African American, she was not allowed. So Marian
sang at the Lincoln Memorial. Seventy-five thousand
people crowded together to hear her music. Marian
Anderson had proved that if you do not give up, you
can make your dream come true.

GO ON

Name _____

Write your answers to the questions below.

What showed that Marian would probably reach her goals?

_____

What events led up to Marian's concert at the Lincoln Memorial?

_____

_____

What do you think this story is saying about what people can do?

_____

Write a short summary of the story. Begin with the main idea.

_____

_____

_____

_____

Read a book about an interesting person. Make a cover for the book. Include a picture and a summary of the book. Share your cover with classmates.

Name_____

Imagine that you are going to take a test on a story about the orchestra. Part 1 will be multiple-choice. In Part 2, you will need to write sentences. Now answer the questions below.

1. Your teacher says you may begin the test. What is the first thing you should do?

_____

_____

_____

2. How will you know whether to circle or draw a line under the correct multiple-choice answer?

_____

_____

_____

3. There are ten multiple-choice questions in Part 1. There are three essay questions in Part 2. Which part will you spend more time on? Why?

_____

_____

_____

4. Which part should you probably complete first? Why?

_____

_____

_____

_____

5. One essay question begins with the word *Why.* What word should be included in your answer?

_____

_____

Name_____

Read the words in the box and think about their meanings. Then read the clues. Write each word on the line where it belongs.

single	assembly	empty	accordion	anniversary

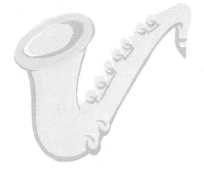

Everybody in school comes to this meeting.

_____

Play me to make music!

_____

It is the opposite of "full."

_____

This means "only one."

_____

It's a special day to celebrate!

_____

Make a "poster dictionary" by yourself or with a partner. On a sheet of poster board, draw a picture to illustrate each of the vocabulary words. Be sure to label the pictures. Display your poster in the classroom.

Name_____

A. Fill in the steps to tell what happened in "Music, Music for Everyone." Start at the bottom and work your way to the top of the stairs.

At the end of the story, the girls feel _____

because _____.

The people at the party think the Oak Street Band plays

_____.

The Oak Street Band gets this job: _____

_____.

Grandmother says _____.

She tells her grandmother this idea: _____

_____.

The main character sees her family's money jar and notices

_____.

B. What do you think the main character learns in the story?

_____

Name_____

A. This band is called the Marvelous Merry Music Makers. Write more names for the band. Make each word in the name begin with the same sound.

_____

_____

_____

_____

_____

B. Complete these sentences. Use as many words as you can that begin with the same sound.

1. A big bear bought _____ .

2. Sam says Sandy sells _____ .

3. My mom might _____ .

4. Pat put purple _____ .

5. Will Willie _____ ?

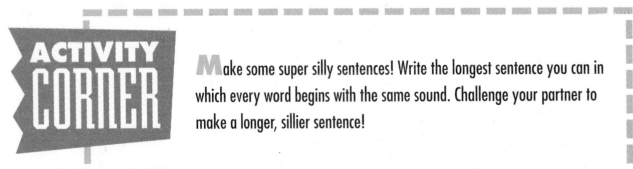

ACTIVITY CORNER

Make some super silly sentences! Write the longest sentence you can in which every word begins with the same sound. Challenge your partner to make a longer, sillier sentence!

Name _____

A. Read the paragraph below. Circle all the proper nouns.

Stuart and Rex were very good musicians. One day

they were invited to play at the Vallco Concert Hall.

Mr. Mohr was the leader of the Shadygrove Bugle Corps.

He was so impressed by their talent that he asked

them to join his group.

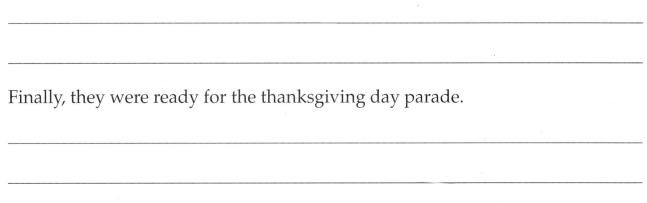

B. Rewrite each sentence below so that the proper nouns are capitalized correctly.

When stuart decided to buy a new trumpet, he went to bell music store.

_____

_____

Finally, they were ready for the thanksgiving day parade.

_____

_____

Usually, rex practiced at lynbrook high school.

_____

• •

SUMMARIZING
the **LEARNING**   A noun that names a _____ person, place,

or thing is called a _____ . In a proper noun, *each*

important word begins with a _____ .

Name_____

Read the sentences below. Use what you know about the sounds that letters stand for, plus the information in the box, to help you read the underlined words. Then read each clue, and write the words on the lines.

The school band was practicing for the parade. The members of the band wore <u>colorful</u> red and gold school uniforms. At an <u>unspoken</u> signal, they began to march. Three boys with <u>unsteady</u> drums were in the first row. Next came the horn players, with the trumpets carrying the tune. The tuba player marched happily, <u>undisturbed</u> by the racket of the trumpets. The smallest member of the band was the last to march. She was the flute player. It was a <u>wonderful</u> sight!

Prefix	Suffix
un- means "not; without"	*-ful* means "full of; enough to fill"

shaky, not steady _____   full of wonder _____

unsaid _____   full of color _____

not bothered _____

Now use two or three of the underlined words to write something about your school.

_____

_____

Name_____

Look at the pictures. Write clear, step-by-step directions
for making a shoebox guitar.

1. _____

_____

_____

2. _____

_____

3. _____

_____

4. _____

_____

Find a book to help you make a simple musical instrument. Make the
instrument, and then show your classmates how they can make one, too.
Be sure to give them clear, step-by-step directions.

Name_____

Choose one of the activities below. Work by yourself or with a classmate to complete the activity.

Activity 1

Read "Music, Music for Everyone" again. Then make a chart. On one side, write "Rosa got an accordion." On the other side, write the effects of getting the accordion. Give your chart a title, such as "Here's What Getting the Accordion Caused." See how many effects you can find. Display your chart in the classroom.

Activity 2

What do you think will happen if the girls manage to fill the money jar? Write another chapter for the story. Tell what the effects of filling the jar might be.

Activity 3

Write an "I spilled the milk" story. Begin like this: "I spilled the milk. That caused a puddle on the floor. That caused . . ." Continue your story, with each sentence telling the effect of the sentence before. If you do this activity with a partner or in a group, take turns writing one sentence each. When you have finished, share your story with your classmates.

Name _____

**Think about what the words in the box mean. Then
write each word where it belongs in the sentences.**

accuracy	memorizing	entertainment	giggle
commercials	performance	nuisance	chorus

They try so hard to sell things in TV _____.

Sometimes I learn the lines from advertisements without

ever thinking about it. I think _____ ads is

easy. That must make the writers happy, since they want

us to remember the products.

Did you ever wonder whether TV ads always tell

the exact truth? Sometimes I wonder about their

_____ . I mean, does your mom hug you

and _____ when you drop spaghetti on the

carpet? Dancing cats may be good _____ , but

does your cat dance for his dinner? Do your syrup bottles

sing together in a _____ ? Personally, I think singing

syrup bottles would be a bother and a _____.

You know, each TV ad is just a _____

by actors. Try not to take it too seriously.

Name _____

Think about what happens in the story "Ramona Quimby, Age 8." Tell about the story by filling in the boxes.

Title: Ramona Quimby, Age 8

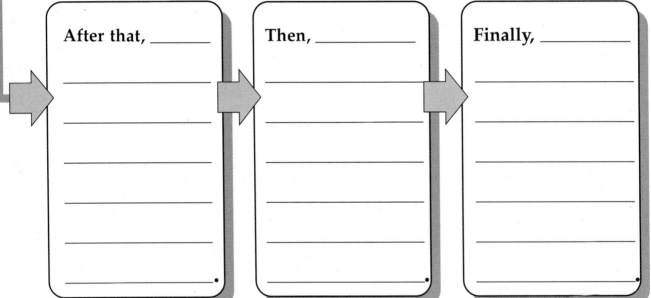

First, Ramona reads the book for her report.

Next, _____ _____ _____ _____ .

Then, _____ _____ _____ _____ .

After that, _____ _____ _____ _____ _____ _____ .

Then, _____ _____ _____ _____ _____ _____ .

Finally, _____ _____ _____ _____ _____ _____ .

Which do you think is more important in this story: the book report or

Ramona's talk with her teacher? _____

Why? _____

_____

Name _____

Read each pair of words. Then use both words in a
sentence. Draw a picture that shows what your sentence
means. The first one is done for you.

1. red, read

I sat near my red tent and read a

book.

2. not, knot

_____

_____

3. eye, I

_____

_____

4. sale, sail

_____

_____

5. hair, hare

_____

_____

Name_____

A. Read the paragraph below. Circle the words in dark type that name one item, and underline those that name more than one item.

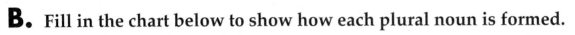

   Shoshana put on her **socks** and **shoes** and hurried to the **kitchen**. Today was her **birthday**. Her **mother** had made a **batch** of **cupcakes** for her to bring to her **class**.

B. Fill in the chart below to show how each plural noun is formed.

Singular Noun	+ Ending	= Plural Noun
sock	s	socks
		shoes
birthday		
mother		
batch		
		cupcakes
class		

••

SUMMARIZING *the* **L**EARNING   Words that name _____ person, place, or thing are called _____. Words that name _____ person, place, or thing are called

_____.

Name _____

A. Read each sentence. Draw a line under the word that uses a prefix or a suffix from the box.

Prefixes	Suffixes
re- — "again"	-less — "without"
un- — "not"	-ful — "full of"; "enough to fill"
	-ly — "in a certain way"

1. We rewrote some TV ads and performed them at school.

2. Janice said sadly that her sink was clogged.

3. Kim pretended to unclog it in a jiffy with Gunk-Away.

4. Harry wanted us to buy Scrubba-Goo to make floors spotless.

5. Ken had a mouthful of cereal and couldn't talk about it.

B. Fill in the chart. Use the words you underlined.

Word	Prefix	Suffix	Word Meaning

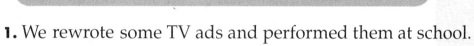

SUMMARIZING the LEARNING Prefixes are added to the _____ of base words, and suffixes are added to the _____ of base words.

Name _____

Read the paragraph and fill in the main idea and details.

Sayonara, Mrs. Kackleman by Maira Kalman is an unusual travel book. In it, a brother and sister visit Japan. They ride on Japan's bullet train. They go to restaurants and a play. They visit a Japanese school. You will learn a lot about Japan if you read this book. But don't expect it to be dull! The author, Maira Kalman, has a good sense of humor. You will giggle at the story. So read this book! Sayonara!

Detail

Detail

Detail

Detail

Main Idea

Now write your own paragraph about a book. Put the main idea in the first sentence. Then write at least three details about it.

_____

_____

_____

_____

_____

Name _____

Read the sentences. Write what the words
in dark letters mean. Then tell what clues
you used to figure out the meaning.

1. **Felines** sound so
   wonderful when
   they purr!

   Meaning: _____

   Clues: _____

   _____

2. It is a very **restful**
   sound.

   Meaning: _____

   Clues: _____

   _____

3. Cats **cleanse** their
   fur by licking it.

   Meaning: _____

   Clues: _____

   _____

4. Old cats sleep a lot,
   but kittens are very
   frisky.

   Meaning: _____

   Clues: _____

   _____

5. Some kittens'
   energy is
   unbelievable.

   Meaning: _____

   Clues: _____

   _____

6. My kitten **slashed**
   our lace curtains
   with her claws.

   Meaning: _____

   Clues: _____

   _____

Name_____

A. Think about the meanings of the words in the box.
Write each word next to the riddle it answers.

Braille	exercises	marigolds	sculpt
dollop	imitating	promptly	sternly

1. We are yellow and smelly. _____

2. If you are always late, you don't do things my way. _____

3. I'm not just paper dots. I tell a story. _____

4. Do this to turn sand into castles. _____

5. We are muscle movers! _____

6. It's not making a copy, but it's copying. _____

7. When I talk, softly is not my style. _____

8. A spoonful is about my size._____

B. Use each of these words in a sentence.

1. Braille _____

   _____

2. dollop _____

   _____

3. sternly _____

   _____

Name _____

Think about what happens in the story "Through Grandpa's Eyes." Then complete the story map.

What John and Grandpa Do	Special Way Grandpa "Sees"
1. _____ _____	_____ _____ _____
2. _____ _____	_____ _____ _____
3. _____ _____	_____ _____ _____
4. _____ _____	_____ _____ _____

In general, "Through Grandpa's Eyes" is about _____

_____ .

Name_____

A. Read the paragraph below. Circle the plural nouns.

My grandfather is one of the smartest men in our family. He has traveled to many different countries. He has many amazing abilities. He built some beautiful shelves for my room. He also knows how to spin pennies so they keep spinning for a long time.

B. Circle the noun that makes each of these sentences correct.

1. Every summer, the seven family/families on our block go camping together.

2. I saw several deer/deers on our camping trip.

3. The flies/fly were bothering us until we built our campfire.

4. Two of the woman/women brought out guitars, and everyone sang songs.

Write a sentence that has at least two plural nouns. Choose plural nouns from the sentences above.

_____

_____

_____

• •

SUMMARIZING
the **L**EARNING   A noun that ends with a consonant and *y* is made plural by

_____.

Name _____

Read the story paragraphs. Then rewrite them on a separate piece of paper. Tell what happens from Jackie's point of view. Use the pronoun *I*. Don't forget to tell some of her thoughts and feelings!

Every summer, Jackie visited her grandma at the beach. They took long walks and swam and dug up clams. Sometimes they read out loud or played the piano at night. Now they were taking their last walk on the beach. They both looked sad.

"Grandma," said Jackie. "I want you to move to the city with us. I worry about you here alone."

"Oh, Jackie," said Grandma, "stand still and close your eyes. What do you hear? What do you smell? Now imagine being on a street at home." She gave her a hug. "I'll miss you. But I just can't give up my ocean!" Jackie hugged her grandma back.

SUMMARIZING
the **L**EARNING   I know a story can be told in two ways:

A story that tells things the way one person sees them uses _____ point of view. It uses the pronouns _____ _____ .	A story told by an outside observer uses _____ point of view. It uses the pronouns _____ _____ .

Name_____

As you read this paragraph from a story, think about the picture you are forming in your mind. Then write details about the way you imagine Grampa, the fishing place, and what happened. Don't forget to tell how things sound, smell, or feel, as well as how they look. Then continue the story on page 51.

I love to go trout-fishing with Dad and Grampa. The only sounds are the birds singing and the river rushing along to wherever it is going. I like to lie on the bank and daydream. But this Saturday, I got to help. When I looked up, Grampa was waving his arms. All the hooks and lures on his vest were glinting like medals in the sun. I guess he was yelling, too. His mouth was moving, but I couldn't hear him over the roar of the river. I ran to get Dad, and we helped Grampa up the slippery bank. His boots had gotten filled with water, and he could hardly walk. When we pulled off those boots, out flopped a surprise. It was the biggest trout Grampa had ever caught!

Grampa: _____

_____

The fishing place: _____

_____

What happened: _____

_____

Name_____

Read these paragraphs from the same story. Picture the scene the words describe. Then answer the questions on the right. **Responses may vary.**

"What a catch!" Dad said. "And just in time for supper, too!" Dad looked so funny, waving his arms and pointing to Grampa's fish.

The fish flopped in the mud. Grampa's mustache twitched as he looked down at the fish. We were all quiet for a moment. The only sounds were the chirp of birds in the trees and the rush of the river. At last Grampa spoke.

"I guess I didn't really catch this big feller," he said. "He just happened to visit my boot." Grampa stooped, picked up the fish, and put it gently into the river. "So who wants sandwiches for supper?" he said.

Why do you think Grampa returned the fish to the river?

_____

_____

What did you already know that helped you answer the above question?

_____

_____

How do you think Grampa felt? Why?

_____

_____

 **ACTIVITY CORNER**

Read a story about an outdoor adventure. Read the story again, and take notes about how things look, sound, smell, and feel. Write about what happens in the story. Then tell the story to a classmate.

Name _____

Read each sentence below. Then answer the question.

1. My cotton sheets had gotten all crinkled in the laundry
   basket, so I was ironing them smooth.

   What can you think of that is crinkled? _____

2. Suddenly I heard loud voices yelling and arguing.

   How might you stop two friends from arguing over a toy? _____

   _____

3. Then something metal loudly clattered onto the floor.

   What could have clattered? _____

4. All the noise was coming from the basement under my feet.

   Where would a basement be? _____

5. I opened the basement door. There, hanging in midair,
   was my shawl, with the long threads of its fringe dangling.

   What object might have a fringe? _____

6. The shawl began bounding up and down in the air like a yo-yo!

   What animals have you seen bounding? _____

7. I shivered with fear until I saw the strings tied to that shawl.

   When have you ever shivered? _____

8. My granddaughter—my son's daughter, Maria—was
   playing a joke on me!

   Whom do you know who has a granddaughter? _____

   _____

Name _____

Think about what happens in the story "A Gift for Tía Rosa." Tell about the story by filling in the blanks below.

The two most important characters in the story are _____.

The story takes place _____.

Everyone is worried because _____.

When Tía Rosa returns from the hospital, she gives Carmela _____

_____.

The two main characters spend time _____

_____.

One Saturday, when Carmela goes to see Tía Rosa, she _____.

Tío Juan calls and says that _____.

At first, Carmela feels _____

_____.

Carmela finally sees that _____.

The story ends when _____

_____

_____.

Name_____

A. Write the action words each picture brings to your mind.

Actions_____

Actions_____

Actions_____

B. Rewrite each sentence. Replace the boring verbs in dark letters with action words.

1. Flora **went** to the market.

   _____

2. Suddenly a large furry creature **went** up to her.

   _____

3. "Grr!" the creature **said**.

   _____

4. Tía Louisa **was** behind a mask.

   _____

Name_____

A. Read the paragraph below. Circle the singular possessive nouns. The first one is done for you.

Uncle Ignacio is my (mother's) brother. My older brother's name is Ignacio, too. I love to visit my uncle's house. The house's front yard has a lawn covered with dandelions. Uncle Ignacio's dog, Scupper, loves to roll in the dandelions. Scupper's bark is very loud, but he is friendly.

B. Circle the correct form of each noun shown in parentheses ( ) below.

I am going to (Aunt Rosa's / Aunt Rosas) house.

The sound of the (car's / cars) motor makes me sleepy.

By the time we get there, the (suns / sun's) rays are almost gone.

My (sister's / sisters) face lights up when she sees Aunt Rosa.

Write a sentence about something that belongs to a favorite relative. Use a singular possessive noun.

_____

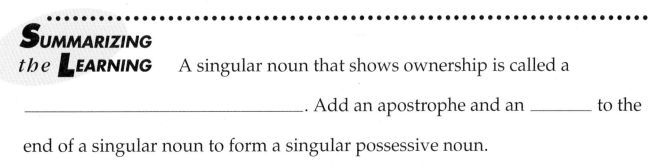

SUMMARIZING *the* **L**EARNING   A singular noun that shows ownership is called a

_____. Add an apostrophe and an _____ to the end of a singular noun to form a singular possessive noun.

Name _____

Read the story below. Then answer the questions.

Every day after Sara finished her homework, she liked to practice knitting. She had learned to knit during the summer. Sara's problem was Mariel, her younger sister. Mariel always wanted to play with Sara when Sara wanted to knit.

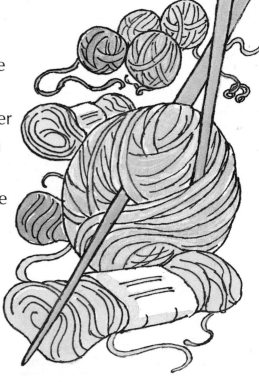

One day Sara had an idea. She went to the store and came home with a big bag. Mariel looked inside the bag and said, "More yarn? Now you'll never want to play with me!"

Sara smiled at her little sister. "This yarn is for you," she said, "and there are some needles, too. I'm going to teach you how to knit."

1. Who are the characters in the story? _____

2. What is the setting of the story? _____

3. What is Sara's problem? _____

4. How does Sara solve the problem? _____

5. Think of another way to solve Sara's problem. Write your solution.

_____

SUMMARIZING
the **L**EARNING   I know that these things make a story:

Who?	**Where** and **When?**	**What** and **Why?**
The _____ are the people in the story.	The _____ is where and when a story happens.	The _____ is what happens and why it happens.

Name _____

A. Read the sentences. Add a prefix or a suffix from the box to the underlined base word in parentheses ( ). Make a new word that fits in the sentence.

Prefixes	Suffixes
un- — "not"; "without"	-ly — "in a certain way"
non- — "not"; "without"	-less — "without"

1. I worked _____ knitting a sweater for Papa's birthday.
(without <u>stopping</u>)

2. I guess I was a little _____ about measuring it.
(without <u>care</u>)

3. When Papa tried it on, it was _____ !
(not <u>believable</u>)

4. Papa just said _____ , "It's the thought that counts."
(in a <u>happy</u> way)

B. Read the words in the box below. Then use a word from the box to complete each sentence.

quickly	quietly	unpack	undress

1. Kevin walked _____ *(how?)* through the dark room

because _____ .

2. So that my clothes wouldn't be wrinkled, I decided to _____

(do what?) and _____ .

•••• A GIFT FOR TÍA ROSA ••••

Name _____

Read the directions and answer the questions.

   You can make a Mexican yarn painting. Begin with a
piece of very heavy cardboard, about six inches square.
Make a drawing on it of a design you like. Put glue all
over one part of the drawing. Lay one end of the yarn
on the glue. Begin at the edge. Curve the yarn around
and around until the whole section is covered. Cut the
yarn and start on another part of the drawing. Use
many bright colors. Keep going until each section is
filled in with yarn.

1. What do you need to make this picture? Fill in the checklist.

_____ ☐

_____ ☐

_____ ☐

_____ ☐

_____ ☐

2. Which do you use first, the glue or the yarn? _____

3. How would you put the yarn on this part
of a picture? Draw in part of the yarn to show it.

_____

4. Where could you get the cardboard for the yarn painting? _____

_____

58   **Following Directions**   Practice Book ▪ **A PLACE TO DREAM**

HBJ material copyrighted under notice appearing earlier in this work.

Name _____

Read the sentences. Draw a line under the correct
meaning for the word in dark letters in each sentence.

1. My grandparents lived on the flat, treeless **prairie**.
   grassy land   mountainous land   wet land   forest land

2. Maybe that's why I love the wide-open look of the **plains**.
   woods   hills   flat land   swamp

3. Every summer, Grandma and Grandpa took me to the
   rodeo to see the broncobusters.
   highway   rocker   contest for cowhands   farmhouse

4. My favorites were the clowns, pretending to play with
   the bulls and the broncos and **mimicking** the cowhands.

   copying   missing   poking   choosing

5. Rodeo clowns still **impress** me with their bravery.

   dismay   affect   improve   push

6. We cooked our meals over a campfire in big, flat **skillets**.
   packing boxes   teakettles   brick ovens   frying pans

7. I helped Grandpa **scrape** the dishes clean, while
   Grandma told stories.
   pat   stack   move   rub

Name _____

Think about what happened in the story "Justin and the Best Biscuits in the World." Tell what happened by completing this entry in Justin's journal.

Justin's Journal

These are things that happened during my visit with Grandpa:

Grandpa taught me _____.

Grandpa taught me _____.

Grandpa taught me _____.

Grandpa told me _____.

At the end of my visit, I felt _____

because _____.

This is what I learned about "women's work":

_____

_____

This is what I learned about "men's work":

_____

_____

When it comes to work in general, I think Grandpa was trying

to say that _____

_____.

Name_____

A. Read the paragraph below. Circle the plural nouns that show ownership.

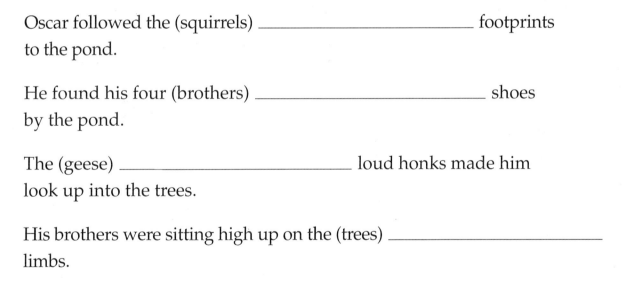

    The chickens' clucking woke Jason. In the distance, he heard a fox's high bark. Jason and his grandfather checked all the animals' pens. By the chicken coop, they saw several foxes' paw prints. Luckily, none of the chickens had been harmed.

B. Write the possessive form of each plural noun shown in parentheses below.

Oscar followed the (squirrels) _____ footprints to the pond.

He found his four (brothers) _____ shoes by the pond.

The (geese) _____ loud honks made him look up into the trees.

His brothers were sitting high up on the (trees) _____ limbs.

•••

SUMMARIZING
the **L**EARNING   A _____ noun shows ownership

by more than one person or thing. To form most plural possessive nouns, add

_____ to the end of a plural noun.

Name_____

A. Read the sentences and decide what the underlined words mean. Rewrite each sentence. Say the same idea in another way. The first one has been done for you.

1. My room was a pigsty, so I cleaned it before Grandpa's visit.

   My room was very messy, so I cleaned it before Grandpa's visit.

2. "Why," Grandpa said, "I see someone has been a busy bee."

_____

3. "I worked like a mule!" I answered.

_____

4. "You're probably ready to tie on the old feedbag," he said.

_____

5. We went to a diner, and I ate like a horse.

_____

B. Complete each sentence to make a comparison.

1. The little girl's hair was as red as _____.

2. I get as mad as a wet hen when _____.

3. Grandpa is a tiger when _____.

4. My room was as messy as _____.

SUMMARIZING the LEARNING   Writers use figurative language to make their writing

_____.

Name _____

A. Read each sentence. Draw a line under the word
that begins with the prefix *pre-* or *re-* or ends with
the suffix *-ful* or *-ly*.

1. I am honestly trying to help more with the housework.

2. For example, yesterday I set the washing machine on "prewash."

3. You know how you have to premeasure the soap powder?

4. Well, I guess I wasn't careful when I read the directions.

5. Soap bubbles nearly filled the laundry room!

6. Then of course I had to rewash all those clothes.

B. Write each word you underlined and its meaning.
The prefixes and suffixes in the box may help you.

Word   Meaning

1. _____   _____

2. _____   _____

3. _____   _____

4. _____   _____

5. _____   _____

6. _____   _____

Prefixes	Suffixes
re- — "again" pre- — "before"	-ly — "in a certain way" -ful — "full of; enough to fill"

Name _____

A. Read the paragraphs. On the lines below write the main ideas and the details.

   Real cowboys were different from movie cowboys. They did not spend their time fighting outlaws. Many cowboys got to town only once or twice a year. A great number of the cowboys were African Americans, Hispanics, and Native Americans. Many were teenagers.

Main Idea _____

Detail _____

Detail _____

Detail _____

   On the trail, cowboys spent ten to fourteen hours a day in the saddle. They had to stand guard at night. Cowboys slept on the ground. They had to keep thousands of animals together in a herd. Cattle often stampeded. Riding accidents claimed many lives. And for all this, a cowboy made about a dollar a day.

Main Idea _____

Detail _____

Detail _____

Detail _____

B. Write two detail sentences about movie cowboys.

_____

_____

Name_____

Read the words in the box. Then read the clues. Write
each word where it belongs.

deeds	warriors	custom	gift	tribe

Clues

1. They are the men who are fighters. _____

2. A group of people is sometimes called this. _____

3. This word means "acts" or "things done." _____

4. If you are good at painting, you have a special _____ .

5. It was the _____ to wait for a message in a dream.

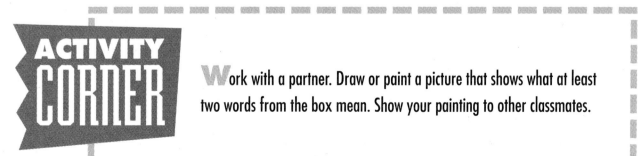

Work with a partner. Draw or paint a picture that shows what at least
two words from the box mean. Show your painting to other classmates.

THE LEGEND OF THE INDIAN PAINTBRUSH

Name_____

Think about what happens in "The Legend of the Indian Paintbrush." Tell about the story by filling in the story map below.

Main Character	Setting
Little Gopher	Many years ago on the Plains

Problem

Little Gopher's special gift is _____

_____ But he is not satisfied with his

paintings because _____

Important Events

1. Every evening Little Gopher looks at _____

   because _____

2. In a second Dream Vision, Little Gopher is told to go to

   _____

3. He finds _____

4. The next day, the people discover that _____

   have _____

Solution

Little Gopher can paint _____

Name_____

Lin is writing a story that takes place in the country.
Help her write colorful sentences. Use the color words
in the box or some of your own to complete each sentence.

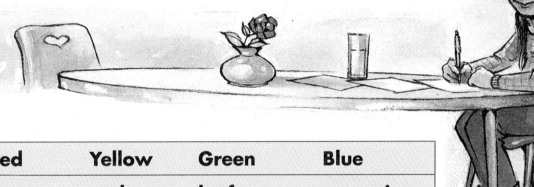

Red	Yellow	Green	Blue
flame	amber	leaf	turquoise
ruby	gold	emerald	sky
cherry	lemon	forest	baby blue

1. The sun warmed the meadow's (green) _____ grass.

2. Tiny (red) _____ and (yellow) _____ flowers sprinkled
the ground.

3. The color of the dress the girl wore was (blue) _____.

4. A large butterfly fluttered by, showing off its black and (yellow)

_____ wings.

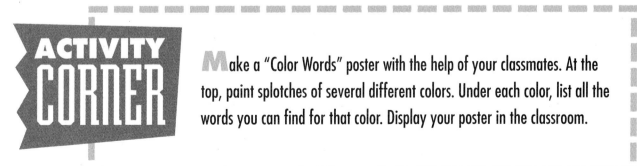

ACTIVITY CORNER

Make a "Color Words" poster with the help of your classmates. At the
top, paint splotches of several different colors. Under each color, list all the
words you can find for that color. Display your poster in the classroom.

Name_____

A. Read the paragraph below. Look closely at the underlined pronouns. Find and circle the word or words each pronoun replaces. Then draw an arrow from the pronoun to the word or words it replaces. The first one has been done for you.

(Jacinto) is an artist from Mexico. He paints pictures of people. Jacinto painted a picture of my grandparents. In the picture, they are sitting down. My grandmother is wearing a silver necklace. She gave it to my mother.

B. Complete the paragraph below by writing a pronoun on each line.

One day, a jeweler cleaned the necklace. The jeweler said _____ was very valuable. Now, my mother keeps this necklace and her other jewels safe. _____ are in a bank. Someday, my sister and I will get to see them. Maybe my mother will let _____ try on the necklace.

• •

SUMMARIZING
the **L**EARNING   A word that replaces one or more nouns is called a

_____. *I*, _____, and *it* are

_____ pronouns. _____, and *them* are

_____ pronouns.

Name_____

Read the paragraphs and answer the questions.

Little Elk awoke suddenly and opened his eyes. It was still night. Outside his tepee he heard a soft, scratching noise.

1. What do you think is making the noise? _____

Little Elk was curious. What could be making that noise? Quietly he crawled to the tepee opening and peered outside. He saw a small, dark shape, a bushy tail, and two huge eyes.

2. What do you think Little Elk saw? _____

_____

3. What made you think this was a good guess? _____

_____

4. What do you think Little Elk will do next? Tell why. _____

_____

ACTIVITY CORNER

Tell a group of classmates a story you have read recently or one you have made up. Pause often and ask your listeners to predict what will happen next. Keep track of how often they are correct!

Name_____

Read this story beginning. Then write your responses
on the notebooks below.

Little Flower was tired from playing with her friends.
While she was resting beside her family's tepee, she saw
a brown rabbit run into the woods. Little Flower
followed it. She ran and ran, but she couldn't keep up
with the rabbit. Soon the sun was setting and the woods
grew dark. Where was everyone? She tried to go back to
her village, but she was lost. How could she get home?

Setting

_____

_____

_____

_____

_____

Character's Actions

_____

_____

_____

_____

_____

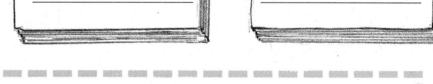

Plot

_____

_____

_____

_____

_____

Pick a partner and read a book together. Then work with your partner to
make a chart with the headings *Setting, Character's Actions,* and *Plot.* Fill in
the information about your story. Share the chart with your classmates.

Name_____

A. Add a prefix or a suffix to the underlined base word to make a new word.

Prefix	Suffix
un- means "not"	*-ly* means "in a certain way"
dis- means "the opposite of"	*-ful* means "full of"; "enough to fill"

1. not <u>usual</u> = _____

2. the opposite of <u>agree</u> = _____

3. in a <u>quick</u> way = _____

4. full of <u>play</u> = _____

5. in a <u>wild</u> way = _____

B. Now write one or two sentences about something you like to do. Use at least two of the words you wrote above.

_____

_____

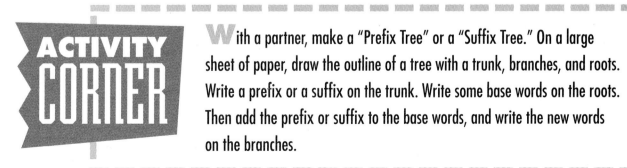

ACTIVITY CORNER

With a partner, make a "Prefix Tree" or a "Suffix Tree." On a large sheet of paper, draw the outline of a tree with a trunk, branches, and roots. Write a prefix or a suffix on the trunk. Write some base words on the roots. Then add the prefix or suffix to the base words, and write the new words on the branches.

Name _____

Read the words and their meanings. Then write each
word in the caption where it belongs.

antiques things made long ago	**handkerchief** cloth used to wipe the nose
cocoa hot drink made from chocolate	**marmalade** jam made from fruit, such as oranges
easel stand that holds a painting	**retired** no longer working
exhibition a show or display	**vacuum** container that keeps liquids hot or cold

The painting rests on a big

_____ in a large

_____ of art.

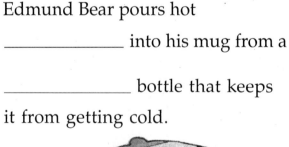

Edmund Bear pours hot

_____ into his mug from a

_____ bottle that keeps

it from getting cold.

The _____ bear eats

_____ on toast for

breakfast.

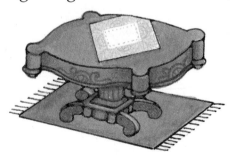

This table and _____

are both very old _____.

Name _____

Think about what happens in the story "Paddington Paints a Picture." Tell about the story by filling in the boxes below.

Title	Paddington Paints a Picture
Setting	Browns' house and Mr. Gruber's shop
Characters	
Problem	
Event 1	
Event 2	
Event 3	
Solution	

What do you think this story is saying about people's

taste in art, or what they like? _____

_____

Name _____

Read the paragraphs. Use the footnotes to find the
meanings of the British words. Then fill in the blanks.

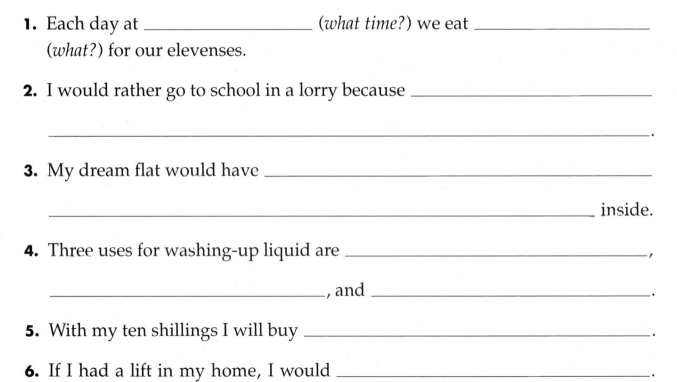

Mum and I live in a flat[1] in London. It's my job to do the
washing up after our elevenses[2] each day. Today we were out
of washing-up liquid.[3] Mum gave me six shillings[4] to buy more.
I went downstairs in the lift.[5]

As I got to the door, a lorry[6] drove by. Splat! There on the
street was a bottle of washing-up liquid! It had fallen off the
lorry. I brought it upstairs and held out the six shillings. "Oh,
you keep the change, dear," Mum said. "Since you did the
errand for me, I'll do the washing up." It was my lucky day.

[1] *flat:* an apartment
[2] *elevenses:* a snack taken in the middle of the morning
[3] *washing-up liquid:* dishwashing detergent
[4] *shilling:* about twenty-five cents in United States currency
[5] *lift:* an elevator
[6] *lorry:* a truck

1. Each day at _____ (*what time?*) we eat _____
   (*what?*) for our elevenses.

2. I would rather go to school in a lorry because _____
   _____.

3. My dream flat would have _____
   _____ inside.

4. Three uses for washing-up liquid are _____,
   _____, and _____.

5. With my ten shillings I will buy _____.

6. If I had a lift in my home, I would _____.

Name_____

A. Read the paragraph below. Pay attention to the words in dark letters. Circle the ones that are singular subject pronouns. Underline the one that is a plural subject pronoun.

My name is Meredyth. **I** love to paint. My mother helped me set up an easel. **She** hangs my pictures around the house. "**They** brighten up the walls," Mom says. My father thinks that **I** am a good artist, too. "**You** will be famous someday," Dad says. **He** is my biggest fan.

B. Write each pronoun you circled in the chart below. Next to it, write the word or words the pronoun replaces.

Subject Pronoun	Word or Words It Replaces

• •

SUMMARIZING the LEARNING   Words that replace one or more nouns in the subject of a sentence are called _____. Four pronouns that can take the place of a subject are _____, _____, _____, and _____.

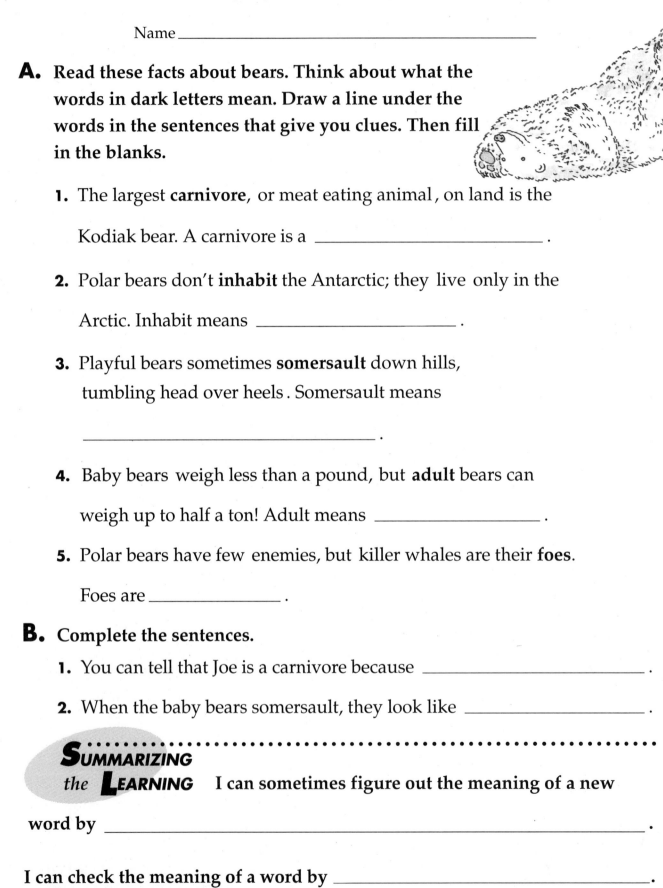

Name _____

A. Read these facts about bears. Think about what the words in dark letters mean. Draw a line under the words in the sentences that give you clues. Then fill in the blanks.

1. The largest **carnivore**, or meat eating animal, on land is the

   Kodiak bear. A carnivore is a _____ .

2. Polar bears don't **inhabit** the Antarctic; they live only in the

   Arctic. Inhabit means _____ .

3. Playful bears sometimes **somersault** down hills,
   tumbling head over heels. Somersault means

   _____ .

4. Baby bears weigh less than a pound, but **adult** bears can

   weigh up to half a ton! Adult means _____ .

5. Polar bears have few enemies, but killer whales are their **foes**.

   Foes are _____ .

B. Complete the sentences.

1. You can tell that Joe is a carnivore because _____ .

2. When the baby bears somersault, they look like _____ .

SUMMARIZING
the **L**EARNING   I can sometimes figure out the meaning of a new

word by _____ .

I can check the meaning of a word by _____ .

Name_____

Read the beginning of the play below
and answer the questions.

*[Theodore Bear's living room. Theodore is holding a big
paintbrush and gazing at a large painting on an easel.]*

THEODORE   This painting business is harder than I thought.
                Ooops! *[He kicks the easel, and it falls over.
                Theodore's friend Harry Bear comes in.]*

HARRY   Oh, you're painting.

THEODORE   Yes. How do you like it?

HARRY   *[looking down at the painting]* It's very nice.
                Ummm . . . What is it?

THEODORE   Well, it started out to be a bluebird, but . . .

HARRY   Well . . . I like that blob over there.

THEODORE   That's where I knocked over the paint can, Harry!

HARRY   Well, maybe you should spill some more. It looks good.

THEODORE   *[He shakes paint from his brush onto the painting.]*
        Hmmm. Maybe you're right. *[excited]* Harry, I've an idea! Get my old shoes,
        Sunny's tricycle, and my squirt gun! This is going to be a great painting!

The characters in this play are named _____ and _____.

Which bear says "I like that blob over there"? _____

Why does Theodore say "Ooops!"? _____

Continue the play. Rewrite this part of the story in play form. Don't forget the stage directions!

"Theodore! Theodore!"

"Oh, no!" said Theodore. "It's my little sister, Sunny. Hide her tricycle, Harry. It's covered with paint drips!"

It was too late. Sunny came in the room and ran over to her trike. "Theodore!" she said, "what have you done to my tricycle? It's covered with paint drips." Theodore just stuttered. "I love it!" Sunny said.

"I helped," Harry added.

_____

_____

_____

_____

_____

_____

_____

_____

Name _____

Read the words in the box and think about their
meanings. Write each word where it belongs in the story.

butler	**chandelier**	**eldest**	**professional**
stumped	**thread**	**tinkling**	

Inspector Bumble here. I am a trained, _____

detective at your service. Today my _____ brother, Harold,

called me for help. Well, of course I set right off to the

rescue! I raced to Harold's home, even though we'd just

had a small earthquake.

At Harold's door, I rang the bell and heard an odd

_____ sound inside. I opened the door to see what it

could be.

Amazing! The glass _____ no longer hung from

the ceiling! Who, I wondered, could have taken such a thing?

Perhaps the piles of broken glass on the floor would give a clue!

Just then, a man in a servant's uniform said, "Your coat is

ripped, sir." He held out a spool of _____ on a silver tray.

"Aha!" I said. "I knew I'd find the answer! I've never

been _____ yet! The _____ did it!"

"I beg your pardon, sir," said the servant, "but I have

never torn a coat in my life!"

Name _____

Think about what happens in the story "Piggins." Retell
the story by filling in the story frame below.

The story takes place _____.

_____,_____, and _____

are important characters in the story. A problem happens

when _____.

The problem is solved when _____

_____. At the end

of the story, Mrs. Reynard _____

_____.

Can you tell the story of "Piggins" in one sentence? Try it below!

_____

_____

_____

Name_____

A. Draw a line under the word in each sentence that represents a sound.

1. The clatter of plates woke me up.

2. Then I thought I heard a quack.

3. I pressed a button beside my bed to buzz for the butler.

4. His new shoes creaked as he climbed the stairs.

5. The mouse squeaked in the kitchen.

B. Draw pictures. Show what is making each sound. Then write a sentence about each drawing.

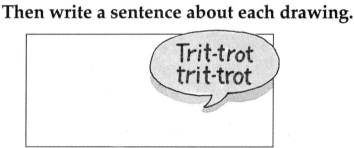

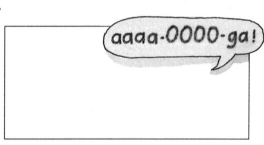

1. _____

_____

2. _____

_____

3. _____

_____

4. _____

_____

Name_____

A. Read the paragraph below. Circle the object pronouns.

Last night, the butler heard a knock at the front

door. He went to answer it. Outside was a mysterious-

looking man in a long cape. The butler stared at him

with wide eyes. "May I help you?" asked the butler.

B. Circle the object pronoun in parentheses ( ) that can
replace the underlined word or words in each sentence.

1. Mom asked <u>Jeff and Lily</u> to help her wash the dishes. *(me/them)*

2. Chris must ask <u>the teacher</u> for permission to leave the room. *(us/him)*

3. Tariq helped <u>Ruby and me</u> with our homework. *(us/you)*

4. Willie studied for <u>the test</u> until 8:30 last night. *(it/him)*

5. Min baked a cake for <u>Mrs. Kim</u>. *(you/her)*

Write two sentences about a mystery you solved or a lost item you found.
Use at least one object pronoun.

_____

_____

•••

SUMMARIZING
the **L**EARNING   A pronoun that follows an action verb or a word like *for* or *at*

is called an _____. Three object pronouns are _____,

_____, and _____.

Name_____

A. Read each book title. Write *fiction* or *nonfiction* to
show what kind of book it probably is.

1. _____ *How to Hire a Butler*

2. _____ *The Butler Did It! An Inspector Rat Mystery*

3. _____ *Mystery Novels: A Guide to Writing*

4. _____ *The Case of the Stolen Gym Shorts*

5. _____ *The Detective and the Dirty Dog*

B. These books might be fiction or nonfiction. Read
the sentences. Write *fiction* or *nonfiction* on the line.
One is done for you.

1. *Third-Grade Detective*

_____nonfiction_____ Jill Masters, a third-grade student, solved a
mystery with a science experiment.

_____fiction_____ Murray wore his disguise to school.

2. *The Train Robbery*

_____ The Tinytown Tinsel Train arrived on time at the
twisted trestle on Tuesday at 2:20.

_____ In 1992, four men managed to derail an Amtrak
train and made off with two million dollars.

**SUMMARIZING
the LEARNING** Stories that tell about made-up people, things, or

events are _____. Selections that tell about

true things or real people are _____.

Name _____

Read the story and answer the questions.

> The famous detective, Mr. P. Eye, came to dinner. He brought along his assistant Higgins. Suddenly . . . CRASH! The chandelier fell. "Aha! Foul play!" said Eye.
>
> "The rope was frayed, sir," said Higgins. He held up the rope.
>
> CLINK! Someone dropped a knife on the tablecloth. "Aha! Blood on the blade!" said Eye.
>
> "Ketchup, sir," said Higgins.
>
> BLINK! The lights went out!

1. Who will speak next? _____

2. Why do you think so? _____

_____

3. What will Mr. Eye think made the lights go out? _____

_____

4. Why do you think so? _____

_____

5. What may Higgins say made the lights go out? _____

_____

6. If there is a crime, who do you think will solve it? _____

_____

_____

7. What other event might happen at the dinner? _____

_____

Name _____

A. Read the story. On the lines below write the
meanings of the words in dark letters.

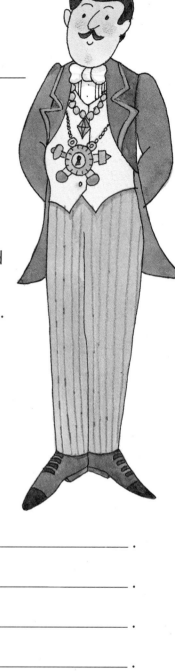

There were a hundred guests. Their laughing and talking
made quite a **commotion**. Mrs. Uppercrust arrived in a
fancy **carriage** pulled by four horses. Her necklace was
covered with diamonds, rubies, and other **gems.** All around
her were wires and gears and pulleys and buttons. The
strange machine whirred and ticked. "Goodness!" said Mrs.
Peacock. "What's that **contraption**?"

"It keeps my necklace safe," Mrs. Uppercrust answered.
"I don't want a thief to **filch** it!"

"But, my dear, how will you dance?" Mrs. Peacock
summoned her butler by ringing a little bell. He came right
away, and she hung the necklace and the machine around
his neck. "There!" she said. "Aren't butlers just wonderful!"

1. A **commotion** is _____.

2. A **carriage** is _____.

3. **Gems** are _____.

4. A **contraption** is _____.

5. **Filch** means _____.

6. **Summoned** means _____.

B. Complete the sentences.

1. I'd like to have a special bell to **summon** _____.

2. If you want to hear a **commotion**, _____.

3. I'd like to invent a **contraption** that _____.

Name_____

A. Read the sentences. Draw a line under the correct meaning for the word in dark letters in each sentence.

1. Dad and Grandpa were **outdoorsmen** who loved to hike and camp.

people who like being in nature   people who like building things

people who like answering doors   people who like being inside

2. When we went **canoeing** down the Blue River, I helped paddle.

hiking   swimming

riding in a certain kind of boat   driving a certain kind of car

3. If it rained, I just put on my **poncho** and kept going.

waterproof hat   waterproof boots   waterproof cloak   waterproof pants

4. We used a **compass** to find our way through the woods.

instrument for measuring distance   instrument for sending messages

instrument for telling time   instrument for telling directions

5. The only time Dad ever got **grumpy** was when I dropped his compass in the river.

happy   grouchy   silly   greedy

B. Write a paragraph to answer the question. Use the words in the box.

grumpy	**poncho**	**compass**

What should outdoorsmen do if they get lost in the rain?

_____

_____

_____

Name _____

Think about what happens in the story "The Lost Lake." Fill in the story map to retell the story.

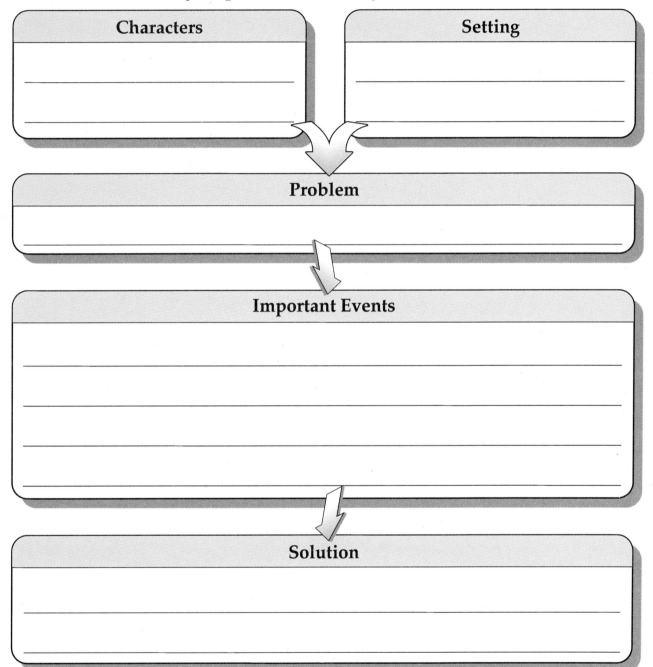

Characters

_____

_____

_____

Setting

_____

_____

Problem

_____

_____

Important Events

_____

_____

_____

_____

Solution

_____

_____

How do Luke and his dad change during the story? _____

_____

••• THE LOST LAKE •••

Name _____

A. Read the words in the box and the story below.
Write the words in dark letters where they belong in
the story.

---

alfresco an Italian word meaning
"outdoors"

bon voyage French words meaning
"have a good trip"

clan a Scottish word meaning
"family"

mesas a Spanish word meaning
"flat-topped hills"

mustangs from a Spanish word
meaning "wild horses"

raccoon from an Algonquian
Indian word meaning "he who
scratches with his hands"

wanderlust a German word meaning
"love of travel"

The whole Jones _____ loves to hike and camp. Our

_____ takes us to many faraway places. We have had

_____ picnics in the Alps. We have climbed flat-topped

_____ in Mexico. We like to watch wild animals on our travels.

We have seen big _____ running across the plains. We have

watched furry _____ washing their meals in a stream.

You can come along with us if you want to. If not, get ready to say

"_____." We're always off on another trip.

B. Use each word in a sentence.

1. clan _____

2. mesas _____

3. wanderlust _____

HBJ material copyrighted under notice appearing earlier in this work.

Name_____

A. Read the paragraph. Circle the word that helps describe each underlined noun. Then draw an arrow from that word to the noun.

Every <u>summer</u> my parents take me fishing. We go to a special <u>lake</u> we know. We get up before sunrise and carry our old <u>canoe</u> to the water. I love to watch the bright <u>reflection</u> of the moon on the smooth <u>surface</u> of the lake. We bring along three <u>fishing rods</u>.

B. Copy each circled word from the paragraph into the correct column in the chart.

Noun	What kind?	How many?
summer		
lake		
canoe		
reflection		
surface		
fishing rods		

SUMMARIZING

the **L**EARNING   A word that describes a noun is an _____.

Some words that describe nouns tell _____. Other words that

describe nouns tell _____.

Name _____

A. Find the synonyms in each sentence. Draw a line under them.

1. I decided all by myself that it would be fun to go camping.

2. Since I like the outdoors, I was bound to enjoy camping.

3. I got a tent at a department store and new boots at a shoe shop.

4. I read the book *Outdoor Facts* for information on camping.

5. My first outing was a trip to a state park.

B. Find the antonyms in each sentence. Draw a line under them.

6. I learned that new hiking boots may look wonderful but can feel terrible!

7. A tent that feels light at home is heavy on your back.

8. Sunny weather can become cloudy and wet!

9. That first camping trip was almost my last.

10. But when I was back indoors, I missed being outdoors.

C. Use some of the underlined words to complete each analogy.

1. Night is to day as dark is to _____.

2. Clever is to smart as knowledge is to _____.

D. Write an analogy of your own.

_____

_____

Name _____

Read about the lakes. Answer the questions.

    Carol and her mom loved to fish and swim. On
vacation this year, they went to Sunshine Lake.
Unfortunately, there had been a big oil spill at that lake.
The lake was black, sticky, and smelly. Dead fish floated
on top of the water.

1. Will Carol and her mom stay at the lake? _____

2. Why do you think so? _____

_____

3. What do you think they will do next? _____

_____

    Carol and her mom moved on to Whispering Lake.
The water there was clear and cold. A raft with a diving
board sat on the water. The lodge rented canoes and
fishing rods. They arrived on a fair but chilly day.

4. Will Carol and her mom stay at this lake? _____

5. Why do you think so? _____

_____

6. What will Carol and her mom do first? _____

7. Why do you think so? _____

_____

8. Which lake do you think they will go back to next year? Why? _____

_____

Name_____

A. Read each sentence. Write the meaning of the word in dark letters.

1. This summer my family went on a bicycle **trek** across the county.

   A **trek** is _____ .

2. We stayed away from big highways and rode on **secondary** roads.

   Secondary means _____ .

3. Our leg muscles had to work hard, pedaling up steep **inclines**.

   Inclines are _____ .

4. **Panniers** strapped to the bikes carried our food and clothing.

   Panniers are _____ .

5. Our 3,500-mile **route** zigzagged from California to Maine.

   A **route** is _____ .

6. People on the way were **hospitable**, welcoming us to their homes.

   Hospitable means _____ .

7. Some people would rather stay home and watch TV, but I **prefer** a great cross-country bike trip!

   Prefer means _____ .

B. Complete these sentences.

1. The hilly inclines _____ .

2. The packed panniers _____ .

3. Do you prefer _____ ?

4. The longest trek _____ .

HBJ material copyrighted under notice appearing earlier in this work.

SKILLS AND STRATEGIES INDEX